So You Want to Be My President?
The **ULTIMATE** Voters' Guide

Prof. Barry A. Goodfield, Ph.D., DABFM

CONTENTS

Preface

Some years ago I was asked by the Council of Ministers on behalf of NATO (for what was, at that time, the Soviet Union) to train them on how to "read people". During the training I asked various ministers to answer a few, simple questions in front of a video camera so that their non-verbal behavior could be recorded and observed more closely

One of the ministers, a big hulk of a man named Vladimir, sat before the video. I asked him a string of questions designed to elicit responses that reflected his unconscious process.

Me: Say your name.

Vladimir: Vladimir.

Me: Again.

Vladimir: Vladimir.

Me: Say the name of someone important to you.

Vladimir: Natasha.

Me: Again.

Vladimir: Natasha.

Me: What did you call your mother as a child?

Vladimir: Mother.

Me: Again.

Vladimir: Mother.

When I played the tape back in slow-motion, I (and Vladimir) could see that every time he said the name of his wife and his mother, he put out his tongue, closed his eyes, and swallowed down. This indicated a denial of hostile feelings that he felt towards his mother and his wife, Natasha. He was unaware that he was doing this.

When I pointed this out to him, I said, "You have problems trusting women!" He laughed and said, "All men have trouble trusting women!"

I then asked, "How many women work for you?"

He said, "I don't know, tens of thousands."

"I presume that you want your country to survive this economic crisis," I said.

"Of course I do!" he said in a surprised and somewhat irritated manner.

Despite his protestations, the unconscious message that Vladimir showed in his non-verbal behavior indicated that his actions would actually sabotage his plans to improve the economy. Although he said he wanted his country to survive their economic crisis, he would be reluctant to give those tens of thousands of women an opportunity to help.

Had Vladimir's concerns and difficulties been seen and acted upon prior to making him a minister of one of Russia's largest and most important ministries, perhaps the lives of many would have improved and even flourished.

I have been analyzing non-verbal behavior for over thirty years including that of world leaders such as Slobodan Milosevich, Saddam Hussein and Usama bin Laden. This experience makes me uniquely qualified to analyze our Republican Presidential candidates for 2012; which allows you, the voter, to make a more informed decision. Given that we are in one of the worst economic crises since the Great Depression, your decision on who to vote for is more important now than ever before.

The Goodfield Method

Over the years I have developed a system that describes the characteristics of twelve basic personality types. I have categorized the candidates in this book into one of 12 different personality types (for a complete list, see Chapter 20).

It doesn't take Sigmund Freud or Albert Einstein to realize that, of the twelve personality types I hypothesize, not all 12 are represented by the individuals running for the White House. There is an explanation simply put, not all of the dozen personalities would find it an interesting or attractive proposition.

Not everybody would want to have an army of busybodies, pundits and partisan political types poking around in your life today and every day since you were born. This is not to say that there is not presidential timber in all twelve of the Goodfield Personality Types.

It is also important to note that sanity, good judgment and even mental health are inherent characteristics in all of the personalities. What distinguishes one personality from another is a basic style and approach to dealing with the daily challenges we all face.

Each one of the candidates, who have chosen this grueling path to 1600 Pennsylvania Avenue, has his or her own unique styles, strategies and stressors. What is interesting is that there tend to be some similarities and of course differences in the evaluation of the candidates.

There are some basic assumptions which may be considered in judging the judgments of those who would govern us:

The first assumption is that the unconscious can be seen. Freud talked about it in 1905 when he said,

> "*When I set myself the task of bringing to light what human beings keep hidden within them, not by the compelling power of hypnosis, but by observing what they*

say and what they show, I thought the task was a harder one than it really is. He who has eyes to see and ears to hear may convince himself that no mortal can keep a secret. If his lips are sealed, he chatters with his fingertips; betrayal oozes out of him at every pore, and thus the task of making conscious the most hidden recesses of the mind is one which it is quite possible to accomplish."

Now with new technologies like videos, computers and even the more non-invasive techniques, we can with increasing accuracy use the motivation and unconscious forces operating in us all. Using video, slow-motion techniques including still frame shows the revealing movements of our deeper thoughts and driving forces.

We will examine, with all who would be President, those forces and desires which explain their action and clarify their approach.

The second assumption is that with stress goes regression. This fact is clearly illustrated when looking at a properly dressed person, standing by an automobile, kicking a flat tire or conversely blasting the horn while pounding the steering wheel in traffic. These are human reactions. Nevertheless they are regressive pieces of behavior, which hearken back to early childhood when as children we threw a "fit" when wishes and desires were not met. It is normal to act abnormally. We all find times in our life when we want to hang out that window and yelled Paddy Chavefsky's words from his 1976 film Network the words, *"I'm mad as hell and I'm not going to take it anymore."*

For some the idea of sacrificing their privacy and history for a shot at the White House simply isn't worth it. Some would want to avoid the daily stressful grind and consistent confrontation this road implies. In no way does this signify a character flaw in fact, it may suggest good judgment. People are different and as Willie Nelson says, *"He ain't wrong he's just different."*

You can think of it this way: in Spain there is The Running of the Bulls (in Spanish encierro, from the verb encerrar, to lock/shut up, to pen). It is a practice that involves running in front of a small group (typically a dozen) of bulls that have been let loose, on a course of a sectioned-off subset of a town's streets. The most famous running of the bulls is that of the seven-day festival of Sanfermines in honor of San Fermin Pamplona.

In the United States the closest thing we have to that is running for the Presidency. Both activities are dangerous and not for the faint of heart. The main difference between the two is that the run for the White House can last for months and years, and avoiding being trampled or gored en route is more difficult.

This pack of presidential people are all basically "normal." None are ready for the "rubber room." The more successful they become in their efforts, however, the greater the chance people will suggest this is not true. Any normal misstep may be interpreted as a sign of weakness, ineptitude, or simply proof of the fact that they are unfit to serve.

The crazy thing about the primary process is that millions of dollars are spent. Alleged friends, people of like persuasion besmirching the character, honor, and good judgment of their fellow party members. One will be anointed and placed "on high" at the National Republican Convention.

During that time back room deals, nowadays held in smoke-free environments, result in compromise.

Here the candidate, whom I refer to as the "dark elephant", will emerge as the Republican Elephant, symbolizing not just his political involvement and political persuasion, but also his formal recognition by the Republic party. The expression a "dark horse" implies someone with minimal change. In the case of the Republicans I characterize them as dark elephants in this book.

The world stands around with bated breath as periodically happens in St. Peter's Square in Rome, waiting for a white puff of smoke signaling the selection of the next Holy Leader. Again like Pamplona the process takes longer with greater fanfare.

Chapter 1:

Introduction to the Non-Verbal Leak (NVL)

Have you ever wondered why some people are better storytellers than others?

Or why some people are able to lie convincingly, while others are unable to convince their audience that they are telling the truth even though they actually are?

The spoken language is only a part of how we communicate with others. The words we speak are only a part of the message. Our faces show our emotions, our body language shows our mood, and almost every aspect of our physical body in some way conveys some meaning above and beyond what our words actually say.

From our first experience with life we have become tuned in to the non-verbal cues that others give. For example, you may meet someone who "gives you the creeps" or someone who gives you the feeling that you've known this person your whole life. A part of the reason is that on both a conscious and unconscious level, you pick up on the cues that the face and body are sending out. I call this the "Non-Verbal Leak." I'll use the acronym NVL throughout the rest of the book to refer to it. There is also a Body Non-Verbal Leak (BNVL). For the purpose of this book I only concentrate on reading the NVL.

This chapter only provides a very quick introduction into the NVL. To learn more about the NVL in much greater detail, jump to Chapter 19.

For now, in the interest of jumping right into the action, I'll summarize a few of the important terms you're going to come across.

Each person has their own NVL. The NVL is the sum of the Symbolic Levels I will discuss shortly. When the NVL occurs, it represents a double message of sorts. It can show the underlying meaning the person is really thinking or feeling. It happens in three stages, which I call "Symbolic Level of Response," which is observable behavior that is translated to a psychological level in terms of three factors. I'll use the acronym "SL" to describe them from here out.

Symbolic Level 1 (SL1): The Impact

How the person first perceives an event. It is real in the eyes of the person who experienced it. This can be recorded on both levels of consciousness. There are six responses to the impact. See Chapter 19 for a full list of the responses.

Symbolic Level 2 (SL2): The Primary Emotion

The basic emotion wanted to be expressed. This is what the person intuitively wants to do.

Symbolic Level 3 (SL3): The Coping Strategy

The coping strategy is what the person actually does express, not necessarily the way he wants to express it. To learn more about the different strategies people employ, see Chapter 19 – The Non-Verbal Leak.

Finally, to learn more about The Goodfield Method skip to Chapter 19.

I will give you an example.

Let's say somebody questions your integrity by calling you a liar. The SL1 might be shock. It will show in your eyes causing them to momentarily become larger. SL2 might show instantly following the shock as anger. This might show in your tongue moving in and out quickly. The message says; " I'm angered by your remark."

The SL3 might be your lips tightening and your eyes closing followed by swallowing down.

The translation of the Non-Verbal Leak, which may be as rapid as 20th of a second, could be as follows; "I'm shocked by what you just said, it makes me angry, but I will not tell you what I feel."

This "leak" has to happen in the same frequency. It must be observable and testable. It helps us to maintain our image of ourselves, at the same time it helps to keep our jobs, maintain our relationships and keep balance in our lives.

To learn more about the different strategies people employ, and The Goodfield Method see Chapter 19 - The Non-Verbal Leak.

You'll begin to see a picture emerge of the candidates: How The Impact (SL1) strikes them, how The Primary Emotion (SL2) bubbles to the surface, and finally how the candidates employ The Coping Strategy (SL3). As you move through the candidates, you'll see how the candidates fit into a number of categories based on their NVL's.

Chapter 2

Michele Bachmann

A popular package, wrapped too tightly, partially filled with unchecked facts resulting in faulty conclusions

Photo Courtesy of Gage Skidmore (Creative Commons)

"I'm in for 2012. In that, I want to be a part of the conversation in making sure that President Obama only serves one term, not two."
Bachmann to ABC's Jonathan Karl Mar. 24, 2011

Background Information

Current Job	Congresswoman from Minnesota
Previous Experience	• Former Assistant Minority Leader in charge of Policy for the Senate Republican Caucus.
	• July 2005, the Republican Caucus removed her from her leadership position
	• Has never run for president
Born	April 6, 1956
Birthplace	Waterloo, Iowa
Family	Husband: Marcus
	Children: Lucas, Harrison, Elisa, Caroline, Sophia
Religion	Lutheran
Most Recent Book	N/A
PAC	Many individual Conservatives helping elect leaders everywhere (Michele) PA
Total 2010 Receipts (from Dec. report)	$659,595.50

Goodfield Personality Typing

Type 2.1 The Thinker: A Pensive Thinker of Feelings

First impressions

- Dedicated to her cause and beliefs
- Strong, focused, determined
- Somewhat closed minded
- Sees the world as black or white
- "True believer"

Photo Courtesy of Gage Skidmore (Creative Commons)

Non-Verbal Leak (NVL)

1. Eyes open with shock and trance
2. Concentration lines between eyes (thinking of the answer to a problem)
3. One eyebrow elevated (skepticism / distrust)
4. Developed jaw muscles (withheld aggression)
5. Tension around mouth (controlled reaction)
6. Swallowing down
7. Eyes open

Unconscious Meaning of the NVL

"I have pain it makes me angry, I can't show it, so I keep it inside, swallow it down and look for a hole in others logic that justifies me letting it out."

Symbolic Level of NVL

SL-1 Shock, pain

SL-2 Anger, sadness

SL-3 Control by distancing and swallowing down

Five Reasons Why This Person Is a Type 2.1
- Eyes wide open
- Concentration lines
- Developed Masseter
- Tension around mouth
- Jaw shifts

Personality Characteristics

- Capable of an initial Meta-level awareness
- Sends double messages
- Trustworthy regarding her views of reality
- Unfocused, sometimes uninformed, leader with power

Photo Courtesy of Gage Skidmore (Creative Commons)

- Analytical power that can "prove" her points well
- Can be prudent, and contemplative in the face of pressure
- Calculated risk taker
- Natural mediator as a result of a reluctance to be impulsive
- Natural negotiator if she thinks she can win the negotiation

- Sought out for advice and judgment by those who think the same

Commentary Based on Public Presentations and Psychological Observation

This is not an impulsive person. Neither is Bachmann a shy or reluctant individual when it comes to stating her true beliefs.

Bachmann has the capacity to change and to adapt her position when she is intellectually and emotionally convinced of the validity of an argument.

Photo Courtesy of Gage Skidmore (Creative Commons)

Once having taken a position on an issue Bachmann is somewhat reluctant to re-evaluate her initial stance. Her Midwestern roots contribute to her strong belief in the American dream.

Bachmann holds a simple (some would say simplistic) view of the problems America faces today. This is based on her fundamental "Two valued logic."

These simplistic conclusions resonate with those ideas held by the Republican Party's more conservative constituents. The same thing that has sky-rocketed her to public attention and adoration by some, particularly the Tea Party activists, may prove to be her ultimate Achilles heel to some members of the Republican Party and the larger electorate in a general election.

Bachmann has struck a note that resonates in both people and pocketbooks. Her ability to raise funds, which also raises fury in others, will ultimately be the test of how viable her candidacy is with the American people.

Promoting the bad news about another, while failing to present a very clear "better plan," may relegate her to the status of another naysayer in the history of the 2012 presidential election.

Chapter 3

John Bolton

The Dark Elephant Candidate
Arrogance without Ignorance – But, without Friends

Photo Courtesy of US Government (Public Domain)

"Yes, I am considering it."
Bolton to conservative WABC radio talk show host, Aaron Klein,
November 2010

Background Information

Current Job	Senior Fellow at the American Enterprise Institute
Previous Experience	• Former U.S. Ambassador to the United Nations
	• Has never run for President
Born	November 20, 1948
Birthplace	Baltimore, Maryland
Family	Wife: Gretchen Children: Jennifer
Religion	Lutheran
Most Recent Book	Most recent book written: "*Surrender Is Not an Option - Defending America at the United Nations and Abroad*"
PAC	*N/A*

Goodfield Personality Typing

Type 2.3 The Pouncer: Danger on two feet

First impressions

- A "take no prisoner" type person

- Strong, believer in his viewpoint

- Somewhat closed minded

- Defiant when challenged

- Bright, logical, articulate

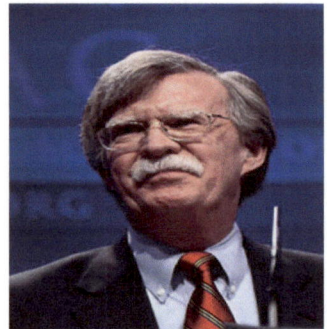

Photo Courtesy of Gage Skidmore
(Creative Commons)

Non-Verbal Leak (NVL)

1. Eyes open
2. Eyes wide open
3. Eyes close (may not completely close)
4. Masseter muscle pulsing and/or tongue out
5. Tighten top lip
6. Swallow down
7. Eyes open

Unconscious Meaning of the NVL

"I am shocked and want to express my anger. Instead I hold it inside until I can find the correct opportunity to express it fully."

Symbolic level of the NVL

SL-1 Shock

SL-2 Anger out

SL-3 Control

Five Reasons Why This Person Is a Type 2.3

- Shock showing somewhat in eyes
- Eyes pulled tight somewhat closed focused
- Shifting of jaws
- Tight top lip
- Eyebrows pulled together (furrowed)

Personality Characteristics

- Powerful person when it comes to facts, data and people

- Critical player in major decision-making situations

- Privately admits to feeling he is living life behind a glass wall

Photo Courtesy of Gage Skidmore (Creative Commons)

- Able to see but limited in his ability to be a full participant

- Often found at the center of policy decisions

- Often found at center of the fray when action is required

- Knows what is necessary to obtain objectives

- Keen observer and insightful about dynamics of situations

- Has skills and outstanding organizational abilities

- When the time is "right," will not hesitate to speak up

- Will notice quickly those who agree and those who don't

- Can choose to be the center of attention showing power

- Sometimes impulsive with the Privately admits to feeling he is living life behind a glass wall

- Often seen as a "larger than life person"

- A "fighter" sometimes viewed as hit in the head too often

- Person that values being direct over what is political correct

- Sometimes shows more guts than brains

Commentary Based on Public Presentations and Psychological Observation

Ambassador Bolton is bright, tough, focused, and generally convinced of the correctness of his position. Depending on one's political perspective you either strongly like or dislike them.

Photo Courtesy of Gage Skidmore (Creative Commons)

Where Ambassador Bolton is concerned, there is little middle ground.

Bolton does not suffer fools gladly and is convinced that the United Nations is one of the largest gatherings of fools. He is arrogant but also well informed on international issues.

His mind is like a steel trap: strong, effective, and dangerous but ineffective when closed. When he locks on to a position, his wit, logic and general tenacity convinces many of the correctness of his viewpoint.

The question is not about intelligence, not about insight, not about skill, but about openness to difference. Often appears more concerned with winning his point with logic and tough talk, then finding a solution with openness and negotiation.

Bolton revels in conflict. As the United States Ambassador to the United Nations his remarks, suggesting that the loss of ten stories of the United Nations building would have little effect on its function, was not the most endearing remark he could have made to his colleagues at the UN.

While entertaining, exciting, and even interesting these kinds of comments raise concern with regard to his reaction to people who see the world differently than he does.

If openness and a willingness to negotiate is a laudable attribute, and perhaps even a requirement for those seeking the highest office in our land, perhaps Ambassador Bolton should rethink how he views and approaches others who see from a different perspective.

One thing is sure, if there is going to be a gunfight and you can't find John Wayne or Clint Eastwood, John Bolton would be a great second choice.

Chapter 4

Herman Cain

DARK ELEPHANT
THE GODFATHER OF PIZZA TRYING TO COOK UP A MAJOR
MIRACLE

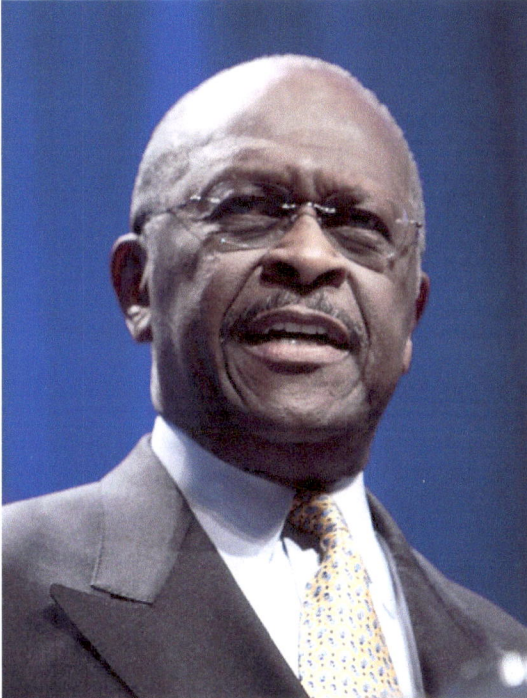

Image courtesy of Gage Skidmore (Creative Commons)

"I am confident enough to be President... After I go through this phase and the decision is yes, trust me, I'm running to win."
Cain on "Top Line," January 2011

Background Information

Current Job	Businessman, Radio host, Columnist
Previous Experience	• Former CEO of Godfather's Pizza • Has never run for President
Born	December 13, 1945
Birthplace	Memphis, Tennessee
Family	Wife: Gloria Children: Melanie and Vincent
Religion	National Baptist
Most Recent Book	*"They Think You're Stupid: Why Democrats Lost Your Vote and What Republicans Must Do to Keep It"* (2005)
Total 2010 Receipts (from Dec. report)	$221,945.00
Cash on Hand (from Dec. report)	$2,246.00

Goodfield Personality Typing

Type 3.0 The Determinator: "I am on my way so get out of my way - please."

First impressions

- Has the simple logic of a business man

- Strong commitment to his solutions

- People's man

- Passionate about change

- Logical in his approach

- Problem solver

Photo Courtesy of Gage Skidmore (Creative Commons)

Non-Verbal Leak (NVL)

1. Eyes open

2. Eyebrows lifted

3. Teariness

4. Eyes larger

5. Eyes closed

6. Eyes open

7. Developed jaws a-symmetric

8. Biting on lip

9. Pressure on lips

10. Swallowing down

11. Eyes open

Unconscious Meaning of the NVL

"I feel the pain of aloneness. I turn those feelings of sadness inward and intellectualize and deny them."

Symbolic level meaning of the NVL

SL-1 Disbelief, denial

SL-2 Anger in & sadness in

SL-3 Intellectualized aggression control by swallowing down

Five Reasons Why This Person Is a Type 3.0

- Eyebrows elevated

- Asymmetrical jaws

- Teary eyes

- Concentration lines

- Lines bi-lateral sides of face

Personality Characteristics

- Frustrated about others' lack of perfection

Photo Courtesy of Gage Skidmore (Creative Commons)

- Hard working

- Seeks symmetry/balance

- Lack of balance causes frustration

- Reluctant to share feelings

- Difficulties with intimacy

- Keen observer

- Intimacy transitory and elusive

- Self-doubt

- Fear of rejection

- Perfectionist

- Strives for perfection in himself and others

- Faults and frailty in others results in primary difficulty in relationships

Commentary Based on Public Presentations and Psychological Observation

Herman Cain is bright, powerful, and orderly with a strong but rigid ego.

Cain has high expectations of others. Integrity is key in all levels of conduct and contact.

Always thinking of how to do and be better.

Photo Courtesy of Gage Skidmore (Creative Commons)

Cain has the power to stay engaged through hard times and power to disengage if his expectations are not lived up to by others.

Cain is understanding, compassionate and capable of giving up what's here and now for what might come later.

Herman Cain's approach to the presidency reflects his history as a successful businessman. He sees a problem as a challenge that is surmountable with common sense, good will, and most of all, hard work.

This common sense approach has historically led to faulty conclusions. Common sense is that which tells you the world is flat. The global economy and geopolitical factors seem impervious to the boundaries of the United States and Herman Cain's world.

Cain's pizza parlor mentality, while creating a great taste in the minds of many, may prove unpalatable when offered to a larger population with different tastes and perspectives on what's good for the American people.

Cain is a problem solver who has been successful at addressing the basic needs of people. The question that his campaign faces is: Does his practical solutions to complex problems resonate with people who are daily being told that there are no simple answers to complex problems?

Regardless of the success of his campaign for President, no one will convince him that common sense and hard work is not the solution to many of the problems faced by America today.

His lack of political sophistication has forced him to eat more of his own words, than he ate pizza as the "Don" of Godfather Pizza. His belief in himself and his message will never, however, result in him eating humble pie.

Cain delivers an inspiring message which harkens back to the kind of campaign Harry Truman and his hero Ronald Reagan would have admired.

Chapter 5

🚫 **Chris Christie**

THE DARK ELEPHANT CANDIDATE

JERSEY SHORE WITH COMMON SENSE AND CLASS

Photo Courtesy of Gage Skidmore (Creative Commons)

Note: *He says he will not run for office as of September 28*

Background Information

Current Job	Governor of New Jersey
Previous Experience	• Former chief federal law enforcement officer in New Jersey • Has never run for President
Born	September 6, 1962
Birthplace	Newark, New Jersey - raised in Livingston, New Jersey
Family	Wife: Mary Pat Children: Andrew, Sarah, Patrick, and Bridget
Religion	Roman Catholic
Most Recent Book	*This American Family* (2010)
PAC	N/A

Goodfield Personality Typing

Type 3.2 Inquisitor: "I am on my way so get out of my way - please"

First impressions
- Charismatic/funny
- The guy next door
- Ready to fight
- A "Can do" guy
- Strong belief in himself
- Family man

Photo Courtesy of Gage Skidmore (Creative Commons)

Non-Verbal Leak (NVL)

1. Eyes open
2. Eyes shiny
3. Shifting of jaws
4. Eyebrow(s) up
5. Building up pressure around mouth
6. Mouth open
7. Showing teeth
8. Mouth closed
9. Eyes closing, but not completely (distrust)
10. Swallow down
11. Eyes open

Unconscious Meaning of the NVL

"I feel pain and fear, and become angry. My question is: "Shall I show this - or distance myself."

Symbolic Level of the NVL

SL-1 Pain, fear

SL-2 Anger out

SL-3 Cynicism, swallowing down, CER

Five Reasons Why This Person Is a Type 3.2

- One eyebrow up
- Shifting of jaws (smoking behavior)
- Eyes closing, but not completely (distrust)
- Difference between left and right side of mouth
- Blocked breathing

Personality Characteristics

- Focused

- Intense

- Distrusting

- Relentless questioner

- Power to influence

- Persuasive

- Attracted to power

- Comfortable in a leadership position

- Trustworthy

- Arrogant

- Tough

- Strong

- Self-concept: "winner"

- History of risk-taking

- Quintessential leader

- Self-assured

- Revels in controversy

- Determined

- Often hostile

- Intelligent and educated

- Calm in crises

Photo Courtesy of Iowapolitics.com (Creative Commons)

Commentary Based on Public Presentations and Psychological Observation

Chris Christie was named U.S. Attorney for the District of New Jersey in 2002. As the Chief Federal Law Enforcement officer in New Jersey, he earned praise from leaders in both parties. Christie drew national attention for his efforts in battling political corruption, corporate crime, human trafficking, gangs, terrorism and polluters.

Photo Courtesy of Hoboken Condos (Creative Commons)

Regardless of party affiliation or political influence, when laws were broken, he took action. His office racked up an astonishing record - winning convictions or guilty pleas from over 130 public officials - both Republican and Democrat - without losing a single case. Christie is also a trustworthy individual who surrounds himself with people who look to him for leadership or guidance.

This person is the quintessential leader: Self-assured, calm in crisis, revealing controversy with a sense of direction that assumes that his perception of the facts is the undeniable truth itself. Christie has a history of risk taking and often a series of successes that validate the decisions behind the risks taken. Add intelligence and education to him and the sky is the limit.

Governor Christie is intense, focused and skeptical. He is a person who asks a succession of relentless and searching questions. This barrage of questions can be perceived as a hostile interrogation. For the Inquisitor, however, the questions are designed to help him determine the truth and satisfy his curiosity.

Christie is tough, strong and determined. He sees himself, and is often seen by others, as a winner. He has real power to lead.

Christie influences and persuades others to endorse his positions or viewpoints in general. This person migrates toward power and is very comfortable in leadership positions.

There has been an increasing pressure for him to run for Presidency. But still his remarks, recently made at the Reagan Presidential Library, indicate his continue reluctance to toss his hat into the ring.

His "down home guy next door" manner says something about the Republican Party's desire for a certain image in their candidate to challenge President Obama.

Chapter 6

Newt Gingrich

"A MAN TOO SMART FOR AMERICA'S BRITCHES"

Photo Courtesy of Gage Skidmore (Creative Commons)

"I'm announcing my candidacy for President of the United States, because I believe we can return America to hope and opportunity, to full employment, to real security, to an American energy program, to a balanced budget."
Gingrich announcement video, May 11, 2011

Background Information

Current Job	Chairman, American Solutions for Winning the Future, Center for Health Transformation
Previous Experience	• Former Speaker of the U.S. House • Has never run for President
Born	June 17, 1943
Birthplace	Harrisburg, Pennsylvania
Family	Wife: Callista Children: Kathy and Jackie (with first ex-wife, Jackie Battley)
Religion	Roman Catholic (formerly Baptist; converted in March'09)
Most Recent Book	*"To Save America: Stopping Obama's Secular-Socialist Machine"* (2010)
PAC	American Solutions PAC
Total 2010 Receipts (from Dec. report)	$736,708.60
Cash on Hand (from Dec. report)	$64,716.60

Goodfield Personality Typing

Type 3.0 The Determinator: "I am on my way so get out of my way - please."

First impressions

- Very bright person

- Very knowledgeable

- Man with great knowledge of history

- University Professor

- Man who does not suffer fools well

- Fish out of water

- Person with wisdom

Photo Courtesy of Gage Skidmore (Creative Commons)

Non-Verbal Leak (NVL)

1. Eyes open

2. Eyebrows lifted

3. Teariness

4. Eyes larger

5. Eyes closed

6. Eyes open

7. Developed jaws asymmetric

8. Biting on self

9. Pressure on lips

10. Swallowing down

11. Eyes

Unconscious Meaning of the NVL

"I feel the pain of aloneness, I turn those feelings of sadness inward and intellectualize and deny them."

Symbolic Level of the NVL

SL-1 Disbelief, denial

SL-2 Anger in & sadness in

SL-3 Intellectualized aggression controlled by swallowing down

Five Reasons Why This Person Is a Type 3.0

- Eyebrows elevated
- Asymmetrical jaws
- Teary eyes
- Concentration lines
- Lines bi-lateral sides of face

Personality Characteristics

- Hard working
- Frustrated about others' lack of perfection
- Scholar
- Lack of balance causes him frustration
- Reluctant to share his feelings

Photo Courtesy of Gage Skidmore (Creative Commons)

- Had difficulties with intimacy at one time (3 marriages)
- Keen observer
- Intimacy can be transitory and elusive
- Does not suffer fools well and "knows" a lot of fools
- Often admired

- Bright

- Strong but rigid ego

- High expectations of others

- Integrity is key in all levels of conduct and contact

- Excellent comprehension and understanding

- Perfectionist

- Capable of postponing immediate gratification for later gain

- Fear of rejection

- Frequently misunderstood

- Powerful

- Orderly

- Always thinking of how to do and be better

- Power to stay engaged through hard times

- Compassionate

- Strives for perfection in himself and others

- Power to disengage if expectation are not lived up to by others

Commentary Based on Public Presentations and Psychological Observation

Newt Gingrich just doesn't fit. Intelligence is very important for one who would be President. He certainly is one of the smartest people running for the office today.

Experience is important when running for the White House. From 1995 to 1999 Gingrich

Photo Courtesy of Gage Skidmore (Creative Commons)

was Speaker of the House. Moreover, he represented Georgia's 6th Congressional District as a Republican member from 1979 to 1999.

Being articulate and able to express complex ideas in understandable ways is important when running for the White House. Gingrich has been a brilliant University Professor. In 1994 he co-authored "Contract with America." He was Time Magazine's Man of the year in 1995.

It is important to have a global perspective on issues if you're going to be President. Newt Gingrich is a noted historian who explains and explores the underlying causality of global conflict.

His personal baggage and brash outspoken style is too much for some.

He has arrogance without ignorance. Somehow that combination gets translated by some as a kind of "Mr. Know-It-All was telling me what I've done wrong. "

His dry sense of humor and intellectual flair seems to be a turn off to many as well. Unlike John F. Kennedy, who bore the burden of brilliance but maintained the common touch in that regard, Newt Gingrich is no John Kennedy.

In an age where image often defies substance and style trumps content the former Speaker needs to say things differently. His appeal to the American voter needs to be a more balanced approach between the head and heart.

Chapter 7

Rudy Giuliani

HAS NOT OFFICIALLY THROWN HIS HAT INTO THE RING FOR THE PRESIDENCY

Photo Courtesy of Jason Bedrick (Creative Commons)

THE RIGHT MAYOR, THE RIGHT WORDS, THE WRONG ELECTION

Background Information

Current Job	Giuliani Partners, a security consulting business
Previous Experience	• Former Mayor of New York City from 1994 to 2001.
	• Ran for the Republican Party nomination in the 2008 United States Presidential election
Born	May 28, 1944
Birthplace	Brooklyn, New York
Family	Wife: Judith Nathan Children: Andrew and Caroline (with second wife, Donna Hanover)
Religion	Roman Catholic
Most Recent Book	*Leadership (2002)*

Goodfield Personality Typing

Type 2.3 Pouncer: "Danger on two feet"

First impressions

- Charismatic

- Real "New Yorker" non-apologetic

- Romantic

- Good guy to have on your side

- Bad guy to have against you

Photo Courtesy of Bill Fish - Victory NH (Creative Commons)

Non-Verbal Leak (NVL)

1. Eyes open
2. Eyes wide open
3. Eyes close (may not completely close)
4. Masseter muscle pulsing and/or tongue out
5. Tighten top lip
6. Swallow down
7. Eyes open

Unconscious Meaning of the NVL

"I am shocked and want to express my anger; instead I hold it inside until I can find the correct opportunity to express it fully."

Symbolic Level of the NVL

SL-1 Shock

SL-2 Anger out

SL-3 Control by biting down, CER

Five Reasons Why This Person Is a Type 2.3

- Shock showing somewhat in eyes
- Eyes pulled tight somewhat closed focused
- Shifting of jaws
- Tight top lip
- Eyebrows pulled together (furrowed)

Personality Characteristics

- Powerful person when it comes to facts, data and people

- Critical player in major decision-making situations

- Able to see but limited in his ability to be a full participant

- Often found at the center of policy decisions

Photo Courtesy of Bill Fish - Victory NH (Creative Commons)

- Often found at center of the fray when action is required

- Knows what is necessary to obtain objectives

- Keen observer and insightful about dynamics of situations

- Has skills and outstanding organizational abilities

- When the time is "right", will not hesitate to speak up

- Will notice quickly those who agree and those who don't

- Can choose to be the center of attention showing power

- Sometimes impulsive with the consequences that implies

- Often seen as a "larger than life person"

- Person that values being direct over what is political correct

- Sometimes shows more guts than brains

Commentary Based on Public Presentations and Psychological Observation

A Democrat and Independent in the 1970s, and a Republican since the 1980s, Giuliani served in the United States Attorney's Office for the Southern District of New York, eventually becoming U.S. Attorney. He prosecuted a number of high-profile cases, including ones against organized crime and Wall Street financiers.

Photo Courtesy of Bill Fish - Victory NH
(Creative Commons)

Giuliani served two terms as Mayor of New York City, running on both the Republican and Liberal lines. He was credited with initiating improvements and with a reduction in crime, pressing the city's quality of life initiatives. He ran for the United States Senate in 2000 but withdrew due to being diagnosed with prostate cancer and revelations about his personal life. Giuliani gained international attention for his leadership, during and after the September 11, 2001 attacks on the World Trade Center.

For those actions, Giuliani received an honorary knighthood from Queen Elizabeth II in 2002.

Rudy Giuliani is not just a New Yorker; he is a Brooklyn New Yorker, with all the stereotyped characteristics that implies.

He is bright, tough and "street smart".

Giuliani is a polarizing personality who freely accepts this role. Weather in the role of a "crime busting" Federal Prosecutor or Mayor of the "Big Apple," Rudy Giuliani has captured the imagination of America.

The difference between the left side and right side of his mouth is illustrative of the differences that lie deep within, this simple yet complex individual. One side reveals the irony in the way he looks at life. While the other side reveals the "Brooklyn street fighter."

Underneath that tough exterior beats the heart of a hopeless romantic. Giuliani's history of risk taking behavior coupled with this romanticism and failure in relationships would have been a career crusher for anyone with a thinner skin and weaker ego.

Giuliani is a "people person" and a man of passion. He would rather do what he thinks is right over doing what he thinks is politically advantageous. This is the good news and the bad news about him.

To the extent that seeking the Presidency implies adhering to a prescribed formula designed to get elected, the good news about his spontaneous lifestyle may become an impediment and ultimately a critical liability.

America's Major may remain just that and not the next President unless focus and commitment become part of that larger-than-life personality.

Chapter 8

Jon Huntsman

A WONDERFUL PERSON KISSED BY THE WRONG WASHINGTON PRINCE

Photo Courtesy of David Keller (Creative Commons)

"Things are moving pretty quickly. Whatever timeline one is looking at can't be more than a couple of months."
Huntsman said to reporters after meeting with South Carolina Gov. Nikki Haley, May 7, 2011

Background Information

Current Job	TBD
Previous Job	• Former U.S. Ambassador to China • Has never run for president
Born	June 24, 1961
Birthplace	Palo Alto, Calif.
Family	Wife: Mary Kaye Children: Mary Anne, Abigail, Elizabeth, Jon, William, Gracie Mei, and Asha Bharati
Religion	Mormon
Most Recent Book	N/A
PAC	Horizon PAC
Note	A day after announcing his campaign for President, Huntsman raised $1.2 million. Huntsman raised approximately $4.1 million in the first weeks of his candidacy. Huntsman, who has a net-worth speculated to be between $11 million and $74 million, was reported to have contributed "less than half" of his campaign's $4.1 million haul.

Goodfield Personality Typing

Type 3.0 The Determinator: "I am on my way so get out of my way - please."

First impressions

- Articulate person
- Very informed man
- Kind, gentle person
- Principled person
- Highly intelligent
- Well educated man with integrity
- Lacks humor

Photo Courtesy of Iowapolitics.com (Creative Commons)

Non-Verbal Leak (NVL)

1. Eyes open
2. Eyebrows lifted
3. Teariness
4. Eyes larger
5. Eyes closed
6. Eyes open
7. Developed jaws asymmetric
8. Biting on self
9. Pressure on lips
10. Swallowing down
11. Eyes open

Unconscious Meaning of the NVL

"I feel the pain of aloneness, I turn those feelings of sadness inward and intellectualize and deny them."

Symbolic Level of NVL

SL-1 Disbelief, denial

SL-2 Anger in, sadness in

SL-3 Intellectualized aggression control by swallowing down

Five Reasons Why This Person Is a Type 3.0

- Eyebrows elevated
- Asymmetrical jaws
- Teary eyes
- Concentration lines
- Lines bi-lateral sides of face

Personality Characteristics

- Frustrated about others' lack of perfection
- Hard working
- Seeks symmetry/balance
- Lack of balance causes frustration
- Reluctant to share feelings
- Difficulties with intimacy
- Keen observer
- Intimacy transitory and elusive
- Self-doubt

Photo Courtesy of Iowapolitics.com (Creative Commons)

- Fear of rejection
- Strong but rigid ego
- Orderly
- Scholar
- Lack of balance causes him frustration
- Does not suffer fools lightly and knows a lot of fools
- Frequently understood
- Powerful
- High expectations of others
- Integrity is key in all levels of conduct and contact
- Power to disengage if expectation are not lived up to by others
- Compassionate
- Strives for perfection in himself and others
- Faults and frailty in others primary difficulty in relationships
- Reluctant to share feelings
- Often admired
- Bright
- Strong but rigid ego
- Always thinking of how to do and be better
- Power to stay engaged through hard times
- Understanding
- Perfectionist
- Capable of postpone immediate gratification for later gain

Commentary Based on Public Presentations and Psychological Observation

Jon Huntsman is a gentleman. He has the looks and a smile that says just that. The question is not his pleasantness but how tough he is. Does he have a strong enough bite and sharp enough teeth to see and say that which is necessary to win?

Photo Courtesy of World Economic Forum (Creative Commons

Ambassador Huntsman is a very bright, talented and committed person to the American way of life. He has the poise and manner of a consummate diplomat. The problem is however, diplomacy and poise are not the currency that buys the key to the White House these days.

As former Governor of Utah and former Ambassador to China, Huntsman is prepared to bring logical arguments and cogent thought to what seems like an irrational competition that resembles a mud wrestling contest -- more than the discussion of serious issues facing America today.

Like a butterfly emerging from a chrysalis Huntsman faces the challenge that all aspirants to the White House face: Principal over Party.

What is clear is that integrity and honesty have governed his governance in the past. The good news is also the bad news about this man who would be President. Can Huntsman be, and will he make the transition from international diplomacy to the contemporary street fighter, currently associated with the victors of our recent White House?

Perhaps a clue to his capacity and desire to change lays in his past history. At one time he saw his future as a famous performer in a

Rock 'N Roll band. Through fate and changing facts the rock and roller emerged from the chrysalis to become a political star in his own state and a respected diplomat on the world stage. He will need another successful rebirth if the White House is going to be a part of the Jon Huntsman saga.

Chapter 9

Gary Johnson

Another Mr. Smith who wants to go to Washington

Photo Courtesy of Gage Skidmore (Creative Commons)

"I am running for President"
Johnson announced this via Twitter, April 21, 2011.
Followed by a speech at the New Hampshire State House in Concord,New Hampshire

Background Information

Current Job	Businessman
Previous Experience	• Former Governor of New Mexico • Has never run for president
Born	January 1, 1953
Birthplace	Minot, North Dakota
Family	Wife: Engaged to Kate Prusack (first wife, Dee Simms (m.1977-2005), died unexpectedly at the age of 54 in 2006 Children: Seah and Erik (from first wife, Dee Simms)
Religion	Lutheran
Most Recent Book	N/A
PAC	N/A

Goodfield Personality Typing

Type 2.1 The Thinker: "A pensive thinker of feelings."

First impressions:

- Pleasant approachable man

- Person capable fighting for what he believes.

- Easy-going guy who doesn't like to be pushed around

- Open person

- Honest person

Photo Courtesy of Gage Skidmore
(Creative Commons)

Non-Verbal Leak (NVL)

1. Eyes open
2. Shock video right eye
3. Shock showing in both eyes
4. Concentration lines between his eyes
5. Pressure in the jaw
6. Eyes open

Unconscious Meaning of the NVL

"I have pain and I am angry. I cannot show it, so I keep it inside. I swallow it down and I will find a hole in your logic and let it out then on you."

Symbolic level of the NVL

Sl-1 Shock/pain

Sl-2 Anger/sadness

Sl-3 Control by distancing and swallowing down

Five Reasons Why This Person Is a Type 2.1

- Eyes wide open with shock and old tears in one eye
- Concentration lines
- Developed Masseter
- Tension around mouth
- May have an elevated eyebrow

Photo Courtesy of Gage Skidmore (Creative Commons)

Personality Characteristics

- Mighty force to be reckoned with, when logic is the issue

- Thinker of feelings NOT a feeler of feelings

- Capacity to inspire others with a blend of logic and feelings

- Careful risk-taker

- Natural mediator who is reluctance to transgress freedoms

- Natural negotiator who believes issues can be resolved

- Sought out for advice and judgment

- Meta-level awareness (capable of a "helicopter view" of issues)

- Double messages may reflect his openness to difference

- Reluctant leader that makes him often the leadership choose

- Trustworthy (his openness helps to generate this image)

- Analytical power

- Prudent, and contemplative in the face of pressure

- Open to new ideas

- Not to open to change when a decision has been already taken

- Skilled at selling his ideas with strong logic and statistics

- Withdraws into thinking when emotions run high

- Reliable

Commentary Based on Public Presentations and Psychological Observation

Gary Johnson's personality is that of a walking double message. He has repressed anger that always seeks expression in ways that keep him and, those around him, in an unstable circumstance. His anger is a kind of push pull - anger in, then anger out. He is passive on a verbal level, with a capacity to strike out and, at the

Photo Courtesy of Gage Skidmore (Creative Commons)

same time, deny his actions. When he feels anger, he is reluctant to show it. His general tendency is to give "yes, but . . ." messages. Governor Johnson is a thinker of his feelings, which may make others feel that he is hesitant in expressing his position. This is not true, he is simply thinking about it in relationship to his deeper value system.

Johnson presents an image of a somewhat rigid person. People around him see him as a person who holds back his feelings much more than his thinking. The concentration lines between his eyes reinforce the notion of the value that he places on reasoning issues through to reach a proper conclusion.

He is a person with power but, he is reluctant to show it, lest he overwhelmed another. His basic concern may give the false appearance of a tentative nature, when it comes to decision-making. This would not be a correct conclusion, he is not tentative, he is calculating as fairness and freedom are critical issues for him.

He is skeptical of authority with power, a specially too much power.

His reluctance to infringe on others' freedoms causes others to feel that he is simply an unfocused leader with power. When looking at characteristic facial features, there is shock in his video right eye that can and often shows moments later in both eyes. It simply reflects the intensity and depth of his feelings on an issue.

He is trustworthy but at the same time he does not trust his capacity to deliver on the expectations placed upon him.

It is no accident that Gary Johnson is being referred to as the new Ron Paul in some quarters. He is a man that does not shrink from challenge - whether it is an unpopular cause or a mountain that intimidates most people.

He has climbed four of the tallest mountains in the world, his last being Mount Everest. He aspires to climb them all at some point in his life. He says there is no rush which provides insight into the psychological working of the former Governor of New Mexico.

Johnson is systematic and open to ideas providing they seem logical and reasonable to him. If the issue fails his logic test he will fight that, especially if it transgressing others individual freedom.

He says, "I don't like to be told what to do." His developed Masseter muscles reflect the fact that he has struggled against authority and individuals, who have told him what to do in his past.

His campaign to legalize marijuana will give the Republican Party and, those who might vote for him, a mountain to climb equal to the ones he has conquered himself. He is bright and controversial but, clear in his opinions and quite willing to discuss his views with anyone who will listen.

Johnson is a "Mountain climbing, cowboy boots walking paradox." He says he can identify with the character in "Mr. Smith goes to Washington." He is disillusioned regarding political heroes. Johnson could find himself becoming a hero to the more libertarian wing of the Republican Party, especially if they are "dope smokers." Move over Ron Paul, here comes another rebel with a cause. Gary Johnson is the new kid on the block, who's singing from the same songbook as you.

Chapter 10

🚫 **Sarah Palin**

THE "STALKER" OF THE REPUBLICAN PARTY

Photo Courtesy of Roger H. Goun (Creative Commons)

"I'm looking at the lay of the land now and...trying to figure that out, if it's a good thing for the country, for the discourse, for my family."
Palin to ABC's Barbara Walters, November 2010

Note: *She says she will not run for office.*

Background Information

Current Job	Reality TV show host; Fox News contributor
Previous Experience	• Former Governor of Alaska
	• Vice Presidential candidate, 2008
Born	February 11, 1964
Birthplace	Sandpoint, Idaho
Family	Husband: Todd Palin
	Children: Track, Bristol, Willow, Piper, and Trig
Religion	Non-denominational Christian
Most Recent Book	*"America By Heart: Reflections on Family, Faith, and Flag"* (2010)
PAC	SarahPac
Total 2010 Receipts (from Dec. report)	$3,553,094.79
Cash on Hand (from Dec. report)	$1,328,951.26

Goodfield Personality Typing

Type 2.3 Pouncer: "Danger on two feet"

First impressions:

- Intense
- Fast on her feet and impulsive
- Attractive and uses that fact
- Vivacious
- Has high energy

Photo Courtesy of Bruce Tuten (Creative Commons)

- Self confident and self assured
- Pleasant with a big agenda

Non-Verbal Leak (NVL)

1. Eyes open
2. Eyes wide open
3. Eyes close (may not completely close)
4. Masseter muscle pulsing and/or tongue out
5. Tighten top lip
6. Swallow down
7. Eyes open

Unconscious Meaning of the NVL

"I am shocked and want to express my anger. Instead I hold it inside until I can find the correct opportunity."

Symbolic Level of the NVL

SL-1 Pain, shock

SL-2 Anger

SL-3 Control

Five Reasons Why This Person Is a Type 2.3

- Shock showing somewhat in eyes
- Eyes pulled tight somewhat closed focused
- Shifting of Jaws
- Tight top lip
- Eyebrows pulled together

Personality Characteristics

- Powerful person when it comes to facts, data and people

- Critical player in major decision-making situations

- Privately admits to feeling living life behind a glass wall

Photo Courtesy of Marc Nozell (Creative Commons)

- Often found at the center of policy decisions

- Often found at center of the fray when action is required

- Knows what is necessary to obtain objective

- Keen observer and insightful about dynamics of situation

- Has skills and outstanding organizational abilities

- When the time is "right" I will not hesitate to speak up

- Will notice quickly those who agree and those who don't

- Can choose to be the center of attention showing power

- Sometimes impulsive with the consequences that implies

- Often seen as a "larger than life person"

- A "Fighter" sometimes viewed as hit in the head too often

- Person that values being direct over what is politically correct

- Sometimes shows more guts than brains

Commentary Based on Public Presentations and Psychological Observation

Sarah Palin has a strong ego. If she finds herself in the top leadership position, she will be a person who does not trust the people's ability to follow her correctly. What one will most likely see, when looking at her eyes, are large open eyes showing a kind of shock with distance in them.

Photo Courtesy of Roger H. Goun (Creative Commons)

When it comes to contact, Palin is open to contact, under her conditions only. She is a person who knows what she wants and moreover, what she expects from others. Palin may not speak openly about her thoughts and positions at first but never doubt that she has them. In that sense she may be seen as a giver with a hidden agenda.

Palin is susceptible to any physical or psychological problem relating to the general issues of stress, as she is retentive in nature on some levels. She is very present in her interactions with others and the environment.

Sarah Palin has a strong personality and has a large following among social conservatives. When pressured, she is capable of exploding. She may not be a "media darling" but she gets coverage. This gives her extensive "free" exposure. When she feels anger she may show it or she may repress the impulse and wait for another time and place. What is sure is that she will not forgive and forget. The event causing the perceived wrong will be filed for later use.

Governor Palin is a person who can be verbally cutting and witty in her expression of her basic aggressive impulses. She is a person who feels power. At the same time she experiences distrust and a need to give these feelings expression.

She presents a strong well-developed knowledgeable image often seen as confident, sometimes too confident. She may be perceived as arrogant and sometimes aloof.

Sarah Palin is trustworthy and focused on the rules of the game. And in many cases knows what is expected of her and what is necessary to achieve that objective.

Of course her mixed record in Alaska, Governor Sahara Palin left the job half way through her term, raises justified concern among some.

The Russian expression attributed to Lenin *Doveryai, no proveryai* or "Trust but verify" fits this Tea Party sweetheart to a T.

Sarah Palin and the Republican Party face their greatest existential dilemma. Do we support a polarizing person, who has as many people absolutely adoring her and her Tea Party talk, as she has despising her divisive speech?

In that sense Palin says to her party "Put your money and votes where your stated beliefs are." She is to some fearless, and to others another plain hopeless self promoter. Some might question her "true" beliefs regarding her remarks. Don't doubt her; she is convinced of the correctness of her cause and direction.

Palin is a "Teddy Roosevelt" type of person. More convinced of the rightness of the path she is taking, than aware of the obstacles she faces and creates for herself and others going down that path.

Life is full, and at the same time simple for Palin, as it is for many who see the world as either black or white.

She is the prettiest, most provocative person the party has had in years.

Sarah Palin is like a "stalker" of the Republican party and the question facing the Republicans is: "Do we call the cops or invite her in for a Grand Old Tea Party"?

Chapter 11

Ron Paul

The Dark Elephant Candidate

THE REPUBLICAN PARTY'S JIMINY CRICKET

Photo Courtesv of Gaae Skidmore (Creative Commons)

"Time has come around to the point where the people are agreeing with much of what I've been saying for 30 years."
Paul announces his candidacy on "GMA", May 13, 2011

Background Information

Current Job	U.S. Congressman from Texas
Previous Experience	• Former Obstetrician and Gynecologist before entering politics
	• Ran for president in 1988 as a Libertarian and in 2008 as a Republican
Born	August 20, 1935
Birthplace	Pittsburgh, Pennsylvania
Family	Wife: Carol Paul
	Children: Ronald, Jr., Lori, Senator-elect Randal, Robert and Joy.
Religion	Baptist
Most Recent Book	*"Liberty Defined: The 50 Urgent Issues That Affect Our Freedom"* (2011)
PAC	Liberty PAC
Total 2010 Receipts (from Dec. report)	$183,602.30
Cash on Hand (from Dec. report)	$90,104.20

Goodfield Personality Typing

Type 2.1 The Thinker: "A pensive thinker of feelings"

First impressions

- Dedicated to his cause and beliefs
- Rebel

- Someone who will never quit

- Tough minded and logical

- Major pest to some people

- Smart

Photo Courtesy of Gage Skidmore (Creative Commons)

Non-Verbal Leak (NVL)

1. Eyes open with shock and trance

2. Concentration lines between eyes (thinking the answer to a problem)

3. One eyebrow elevated (skepticism/distrust)

4. Developed jaw muscles (withheld aggression)

5. Tension around mouth (controlled reaction)

6. Swallowing down

7. Eyes open

Unconscious Meaning of the NVL

"I have pain and it makes me angry, I can't show it, so I keep it inside, swallow it down and look for a hole in others' logic that justifies me letting it out."

Symbolic Level of NVL

SL-1 Shock, pain

SL-2 Anger, sadness

SL-3 Control by distancing and swallowing down

Five Reasons Why This Person Is a Type 2.1

- Eyes wide open
- Concentration lines
- Developed Masseter muscle
- Tension around mouth
- Jaw shifts

Personality Characteristics

- Capable of Meta-level awareness

- Sends clear messages

- Trustworthy regarding his views of reality

- Analytical power that can "prove" his points well

Photo Courtesy of Gage Skidmore (Creative Commons)

- Can be prudent, and contemplative in the face of pressure

- Calculated risk-taker

- Thinker of feelings NOT a feeler of feelings

- Often seen as a powerful and very "feeling" person

- Mighty force to be reckoned with when logic is the issue

- Capacity to influence others with a blend of logic and feelings

- Does not trust capacity to deliver, so works harder to prove he can

- Natural negotiator who thinks he can win the negotiation if people listen

- Sought out for advice and judgment

Commentary Based on Public Presentations and Psychological Observation

Congressman Ron Paul is convinced that the Emperor has no clothes.

Paul is a fearless gadfly, who somehow delights in using his logic like a sharp stick to poke in the eye of his fellow Republicans.

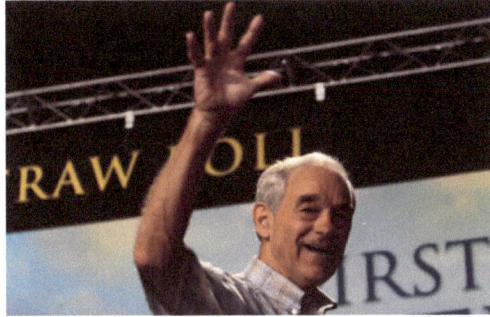

Photo Courtesy of Gage Skidmore (Creative Commons)

Paul is rebellious against what he perceives to be an unjustified use of authority. His sobering logic has driven some of his fellow Republicans to drink. Paul embraces causes based on principle and belief.

Ron Paul is an agent provocateur almost without equal in the Republican Party. The problem that people have with the congressman generally relates to his tenacity and fearless approach, and his advocacy of issues that are inconsistent with the general stance taken by the Republican Party.

Congressman Paul is a "Rebel with a Cause!"

Ron Paul revels in controversy and conflict with authority. His intellectually masked aggression, keen intellect, and disarming logic have been a provocative but winning formula for this aging curmudgeon for years.

One might ask: Why don't you join a more Liberal party or join an independent one as you did in the past? Liberal philosophy is antithetical to Paul's beliefs.

Paul's previous encounters in his former Presidential attempt in 2008 can provide a possible answer.

To be sidelined as a candidate from a third-party in a two-part two-party country, would relegate Paul to an obscurity that his strong ego would not handle well. Congressman Paul remains a national gadfly sharing "The Truth" as he sees it.

Ron Paul is the Republican Party's Jiminy Cricket.

Chapter 12

 # Tim Pawlenty

GOV. SIZZLE LESS: A PROFOUNDLY PRODUCTIVE PASSIONLESS PERSON PLANNING SPONTANEITY

Photo Courtesy of Gage Skidmore (Creative Commons)

"I'm running for president because I can tackle, fix the budget deficit and debt to get this economy back on track. That's what I did in Minnesota and that's what I can do for America."
Pawlenty announces presidential campaign on "GMA," May 23, 2011

Note: *As of this writing, Governor Pawlenty has withdrawn from the race.*

Background Information

Current Job	• TBD
Previous Job	• Former Governor of Minnesota
	• Has never run for President
Born	November 27, 1960
Birthplace	St. Paul, Minnesota
Family	Wife: Mar
	Children: Anna and Mara
Religion	Baptist/Evangelical
Most Recent Book	*"Courage to Stand: An American Story"* (2011)
PAC	Freedom First PAC Total 2010 fundraising for the federal and state PACs: $2,600,000
Total 2010 Receipts (from Dec. report)	$2,096,639
Cash on Hand (from Dec. report)	$154,989.60

Goodfield Personality Typing

Type 2.1 The Thinker: "A pensive thinker of feelings."

First impressions:

• Dedicated to his cause and beliefs

• Man with little passion

• Well organized thought process

• Intelligent and careful in his approach

• Understanding

Non-Verbal Leak (NVL)

1. Eyes open with shock and trance

2. Concentration lines between eyes (thinking answer to problem)

3. One eyebrow elevated (skepticism/distrust)

4. Developed jaw muscles (withheld aggression)

5. Tension around mouth (controlled reaction)

6. Swallowing down

7. Eyes open

Photo Courtesy of Gage Skidmore (Creative Commons)

Unconscious Meaning of the NVL

"I have pain it makes me angry, I can't show it, so I keep it inside, swallow it down and look for a hole in others' logic that justifies me letting it out."

Symbolic Level of NVL

SL-1 Shock, pain

SL-2 Anger, sadness

SL-3 Control by distancing and swallowing down

Five Reasons Why This Person Is a Type 2.1

- Eyes wide open

- Concentration lines

- Developed Masseter muscles

- Tension around mouth

- Jaw shifts

Personality Characteristics

- Capable of Meta-level awareness

- Sends clear messages

- Trustworthy regarding his views of reality

- Uninspiring leader with power

Photo Courtesy of Gage Skidmore (Creative Commons)

- Analytical power that can "prove" his points well

- Can be prudent, and contemplative in the face of pressure

- Calculated risk-taker

- Natural mediator as a result of a reluctance to be impulsive

- Thinker of feelings NOT a feeler of feelings

- Often seen as a powerful and very "feeling" person

- Mighty force to be reckoned with when logic is the issue

- Capacity to influence others with a blend of logic and feelings

- Does not trust capacity to deliver, so works harder to prove he can

- Natural negotiator who thinks he can win the negotiation

- Sought out for advice and judgment do to his skill and ability

Commentary Based on Public Presentations and Psychological Observation

The lines between Pawlenty's eyebrows, what I call concentration lines, and the lines in his forehead tip the world to the fact that he thinks his feelings and plots his passion. The Governor is a man of profound understanding regarding people and their needs.

Photo Courtesy of Gage Skidmore (Creative Commons)

Pawlenty is not afraid to fight and persevere when his views and values are challenged. His character is clearly beyond reproach. And his ideas are very well thought out. There are no accidents in his presentations.

There is neither fire in Pawlenty's water nor scotch in his soda. Simply put, the Governor is boring and the Republican Party would do well to notice someone who slips by many unnoticed.

Filled with great information but expresses his life in lower case without an exclamation mark.

Governor Pawlenty's presidential promotions reflect his awareness of his beliefs as well as Pawlenty's anxiety about being seen as a person without passion. Pawlenty gives the impression of an extremely competent well-organized individual. His "stage presence" masks his accomplishments. There is no "there" there.

Pawlenty is tenacious without boldness; clever without wit and enthusiasm. Simply put Pawlenty is a boiled egg with a pleasantly shaped exterior packed full of content. It's nutritious and healthy, but needs salt.

Pawlenty is convinced of the correctness of his position. He must be willing to suffer these kinds of judgments to let America know, what he feels is the answer to her woes.

Some might call Pawlenty an empty suit. If true, it is well made, well tailored and well designed.

In the end, Pawlenty is still a talented, tedious technocrat.

A day after coming in third place in the August 13, 2011 Ames Straw Poll, Governor Pawlenty announced that he was withdrawing from the race. On September 12, 2011, Pawlenty announced his endorsement of former Governor Mitt Romney of Massachusetts.

Chapter 13

Rick Perry

"NOT THE BRIGHTEST BOOTS IN TEXAS"

Photo Courtesy of Gage Skidmore (Creative Commons)

"I'm not going to Washington, D.C. to be most popular. I'm going to Washington, D.C., to try to save this country from this monumental debt."
Source: Fox News

As a member of the 2012 presidential race, Rick Perry took aim August 15, 2011 at the current occupant of the White House, faulting President Obama for creating barriers to job growth while touting his own record on job creation in Texas.

Background Information

Current Job	Governor of Texas
Previous Experience	• Republican Lieutenant Governor
	• Has never run for president
Born	March 4, 1950
Birthplace	Pint Creek, Texas
Family	Wife: Anita
	Children: Griffin and Sydney
Religion	Christian (Evangelical)
Most Recent Book	*"On my Honor: Why the American Values of the Boys Scouts are Worth Fighting For"* (2011)
PAC	Liberty PAC

Goodfield Personality Typing

Type 1.2 The Plotter: "Ambivalent about being present"

First impressions

- Very nice guy
- Charming towards others
- Honest character
- George Bush look -a -like
- Open but somewhat tentative
- Not forceful in conflict

Photo Courtesy of Gage Skidmore (Creative Commons)

Non-Verbal Leak (NVL)

1. Eyes open
2. Eyes closing, not complete
3. Teary eyes
4. Eyes not focused
5. Mouth not fully closed
6. Lines from the corner of the mouth downwards
7. Tension around the mouth
8. Eyebrow(s) up
9. Block in throat
10. Eyes open (distanced)

Unconscious Meaning of the NVL

"I have pain it makes me angry I can't show it. I am denying myself, that makes me feel sad and also angry, I do not trust myself expressing my feelings and that makes me unsure."

Statement of the NVL

SL-1 Denial

SL-2 Sadness in & anger in

SL-3 Control by holding back and trance

Five Reasons Why This Person Is a Type 1.2

- Trance, but not showing all the time
- Eyes do not close completely
- Eyebrows up
- Tightness around the mouth
- Mouth that is not completely closed

Personality Characteristics

- Goal oriented
- Determination to reach his objectives
- Methodical in his approach
- Dependent on feedback from those he sees as on the "inside"
- Retention of deeper feelings
- Reliable
- Does not live up to the perceived capacities others see in him

Photo Courtesy of Gage Skidmore (Creative Commons)

- Dependability is a strong attribute
- Potential power that moves slowly and predictably
- Capable of reaching long-term objectives
- On some deep level he is unsure about taking independent action
- Non-confrontational regarding personal boundaries
- Capable of defending views and values when attacked
- Capable of deep commitment
- Repressed anger that comes out in persistence
- Prudent but strong when decision is taken
- Goal orientated regardless of price, position, or problems
- Systematic in his approach to problem solving
- Can work alone, but wants other's approval and support on projects
- Blocks himself in debating situations

89

Commentary Based on Public Presentations and Psychological Observation

Governor Rick Perry is a nice guy. He is clear about what he thinks is correct. Perry has a tendency to see issues in black and white. Perry's approach and the success with the Texas economy, when compared to the fragile US economy, have drawn attention from a wide audience.

Photo Courtesy of Gage Skidmore (Creative Commons)

There is no doubt about Perry's commitment, involvement and direction when it comes to what he thinks is best for Texas and what might be best for America. Perry's "hands off the business community" emphasis may be a factor in the economic success of his state.

Perry is open, charming and likable. The question is not about his personal attributes but about the ability to deliver them in a tough political environment where oratory may take a backseat to content and reason. Governor Perry will have to prove that he has the power to convince America of the strength of his personality and the success of his plan.

Although from different socio-economic backgrounds there are some striking resemblances in his non-verbal presentation to that of the former President George W. Bush. At times, there is tentativeness present when Perry makes an assertive remark. Perry's head moves forward and his shoulders move back while giving, what might be perceived as, a tentative smile.

To some this idiosyncrasy may be seen as uncertainty or a lack of assertiveness. It would, however, be a major mistake to interpret this behavior as a lack of commitment to the position he is expressing.

To the extent that presidential politics has much to do with image and style, Rick Perry has the look and style. The deeper question remains: When Perry speaks, does he show the power and ability to inspire a nation in trouble by his will? This Texan, with his simple ideas about what is necessary, might find it difficult to ride into Washington with the philosophy, as the Texas Rangers say, "One riot one Ranger."

Chapter 14

Charles Elson "Buddy" Roemer III

The Dark Elephant Candidate

AN HONEST HUEY LONG WHO CAN ADD

Photo Courtesy of Gage Skidmore (Creative Commons)

"I'm going to be a factor in 2012."
Roemer on "Top Line", March 2011

Background Information

Current Job	Bank President and CEO
Previous Experience	• Former Governor of Louisiana • Has never run for president
Born	October 4, 1943
Birthplace	Shreveport, Louisiana
Family	Twice divorced
Religion	Methodist
Most Recent Book	*"The Roemer Revolution"* (1987)
PAC	N/A Roemer's ideal is a candidate who accepts no money from PACs or Super PACs, employs no lobbyists as fundraisers, and limits individual donations to $2,500, though he said he would keep his own limit at $100

Goodfield Personality Typing

Type 3.0 The Determinator: "I am on my way so get out of my way - please."

First impressions

- Grandfatherly Southern Gentleman
- Simple man with a simpler plan
- Stated "traditionalist"
- "Harry Truman" type politician
- Curmudgeon
- Man smarter than he sounds

Non-Verbal Leak (NVL)

1. Eyes open
2. Eyebrows lifted
3. Teariness
4. Eyes larger
5. Eyes closed
6. Eyes open
7. Developed jaws a-symmetric
8. Biting on self
9. Pressure on lips
10. Swallowing down
11. Eyes open

Photo Courtesy of Gage Skidmore (Creative Commons)

Unconscious Meaning of the NVL

"I feel the pain of aloneness, I turn those feelings of sadness inward and intellectualize and deny them."

Symbolic Level of NVL

SL-1 Disbelief, denial

SL-2 Anger in & sadness in

SL-3 Intellectualized aggression control by swallowing down

Five Reasons Why This Person Is a Type 3.0

- Eyebrows elevated
- Asymmetrical jaws
- Teary eyes
- Concentration lines
- Lines bi-lateral sides of face

Personality Characteristics

- Strong but rigid ego
- Orderly
- High expectations of others
- Always thinking of how to do and be better
- Integrity is key on all levels of conduct and contact
- Power to stay engaged through hard times

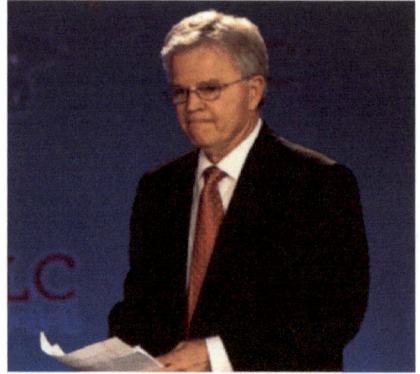

Photo Courtesy of Gage Skidmore (Creative Commons)

- Power to disengage if expectation are not lived up to by others
- Understanding
- Compassionate
- Perfectionist
- Capable of giving up what's now for might find later
- Often admired
- Frequently misunderstood
- Frustrated about others lack of perfection
- Hard working
- Seeks symmetry/balance
- Lack of balance causes frustration
- Reluctant to share feelings
- Difficulties with intimacy
- Keen observer
- Faults and frailty in others primary difficulty in relationships
- Intimacy transitory and elusive
- Self-doubt
- Fear of rejection
- Perfectionist
- Strives for perfection in himself and others

Commentary Based on Public Presentations and Psychological Observation

Former Congressman and Governor Charles Elson "Buddy" Roemer III is a kind of throwback to an earlier time in our country when politics was a gentleman's game.

Governor Roemer is a simple Southern gentleman with a message that comes from his banking background. Don't spend more than you have, balance your books and be a good neighbor to everybody.

Photo Courtesy of Gage Skidmore (Creative Commons)

Politics in Louisiana suggest it is not for the faint of heart or for the naïve. Governor Roemer was neither then, nor is he now. Roemer is charming and honest and believes his simple message and the logic it reflects.

Some might say Roemer is bringing a knife to a gunfight. In fact Roemer is bringing an old-fashioned adding machine to the incalculable economic crisis we face today. His math is simple: One plus one still equals two. And basic principles still apply in relationships, both economic and personal.

Governor Roemer is honest and a man of integrity. One would be foolish to underestimate the quite thoughtful and simple image that he portrays. The way Roemer proposes to fund his campaign accepting no more than $100 in donations and the mathematics Roemer uses to explain how this is a successful tactic, might be something that larger institutions should consider.

Governor Roemer is the grandfather that many would want, the banker that everyone would trust and the politician some might even vote for. What is important is to listen to the logic and values of a political figure from another time, speaking to the concerns of people now.

There is a place in this campaign for a person of this caliber regardless of how you feel about Governor Roemer's message. Honesty and integrity should always have a place in any political campaign.

Chapter 15

Mitt Romney

"THE NUMBER ONE PRESIDENTIAL PASSIONLESS PARTICIPANT"

Photo Courtesy of Gage Skidmore (Creative Commons)

"From my first day in office, my No. 1 job will be to see that America is once again No. 1 in job creation."
Romney announces Presidential campaign, June 3, 2011

Background Information

Current Job	Keynote speeches, GOP fundraising
Previous Experience	• Former Governor of Massachusetts • Presidential candidate, 2008
Born	March 12, 1947
Birthplace	Detroit, Michigan
Family	Wife: Ann Children: Tagg, Matt, Josh, Ben, and Craig
Religion	The Church of Jesus Christ of Latter-day Saints (Mormon)
Most Recent Book	*"No Apology: The Case for American Greatness"* (2010
PAC	Free and Strong America PAC, Inc. $6,300,723.52
Total 2010 Receipts (from Dec. report)	$5,568,466.75
Cash on Hand (from Dec. report)	$796,207.59

Goodfield Personality Typing

Type 3.2 Inquisitor: "I am on my way so get out of my way - please"

First impressions

- Presidential direct from central casting
- Sophisticated gentleman
- Strong somewhat rigid

- Uncomfortable trying to be comfortable

- Has great integrity

- Self confident and self assured

- Comfortable in leadership role

Photo Courtesy of Gage Skidmore (Creative Commons)

Non-Verbal Leak (NVL)

1. Eyes open

2. Eyes shiny

3. Shifting of jaws

4. Both eyebrows up

5. Lines from nose to mouth intensify

6. Building up pressure around mouth

7. Lines in forehead intensify

8. Showing teeth

9. Mouth closed

10. Swallow down

11. Eyes open

Unconscious Meaning of the NVL

"I feel pain and fear, and become angry, my question is - shall I show this or distance myself?"

Symbolic Level of the NVL

SL-1 Pain, fear

SL-2 Anger out

SL-3 Cynicism, swallowing down, CER

Five Reasons Why This Person Is a Type 3.2

- One eyebrow up

- Shifting of jaws (smoking behavior)

- Eyes closing, but not completely (distrust)

- Difference between left and right side of mouth

- Blocked breathing

Personality Characteristics

- Tough

- Strong

- Determined

- Self-concept "winner"

- Calm and focused

- Experienced executive

- Intelligent and educated

Photo Courtesy of Gage Skidmore (Creative Commons)

- Quintessential leader

- Self-assured

- Calm and rational in crises

- Revealing controversy

- Grasps concepts quickly

- Natural mediator

- Seen as hesitant and stiff

- Careful risk-taker

- Prudent, and contemplative in the face of pressure

- Persuasive person

- Trustworthy

- Natural negotiator
- Convincing person
- Master in the art of influence
- Sought out for advice and judgment
- Analytical power
- Subtle charm, yet somehow stands alone
- Can see the "big picture"
- Focused leader with power
- Has the experience to lead well

Commentary Based on Public Presentations and Psychological Observation

Mitt Romney has an image problem and not a reality problem. He has been labeled as uninspired, uninteresting and even boring by some who looked at him as a potential replacement of Barack Obama in the White House. The act of removing a tie, putting on a pair of Levis, may reflect

Photo Courtesy of Gage Skidmore (Creative Commons)

openness but it will take more than that to change his true self-concept.

It is true that wit and wisdom often go together; Mitt Romney appears to be the exception to this rule. His 2012 campaign for the White House reflects a change in image and some would say a welcome change.

Romney may be a candidate for President but he sure is a candidate for a "humor transplant". As much as the political trail to the White House is a serious one there is a place for levity and humor as well.

Another potential obstacle is his Mormon religion. One would hope, in these enlightened times and the more liberal acceptance of behaviors and choices not so long ago seen as unacceptable, that religion would not stir the controversy it did in Al Smith's or John F. Kennedy's time. One might argue that there is a difference between being a Catholic and being a Mormon. Of course this is true but it does not mean that one would govern differently or inappropriately.

The outstanding and unique aspect of Romney's personality and religious belief system is that he does not drink, smoke or use drugs. Moreover he married his high school sweetheart whom he met when she was 15.

His experience as a businessman and Governor make Romney a formidable opponent. There are no skeletons in his closet, at least none that we know. One question remains, however: Is there a warmth and passion that will resonate and radiate to the American people?

Chapter 16

Rick Santorum

A MAJOR CANDIDATE FOR A HUMOR TRANSPLANT

Campaign Photo

"We're ready to announce that we are going to be in this race and we're in it to win."
Santorum announces his candidacy on "GMA", June 6, 2011.

Background Information

Current Job	Attorney, politician
Previous Experience	• Former Senator from Pennsylvania • Has never run for president
Born	May 10, 1958
Birthplace	Winchester, Virginia
Family	Wife: Karen
	Children: Elizabeth, Richard, Daniel, Sarah, Peter, Patrick, and Isabella
Religion	Roman Catholic
Most Recent Book	*"It Takes a Family: Conservatism and the Common Good"* (2006)
PAC	America's Foundation
Total 2010 Receipts (from Dec. report)	$1,564,303.20
Cash on Hand (from Dec. report)	$102,858

Goodfield Personality Typing

Type 2.1 Thinker: "A Pensive Thinker of Feelings"

First impressions

- Non-verbal apologetic/defensive image
- "True believer"
- Carries a lot of anxiety
- Person who justifies his actions

- Passive aggressive regarding expression of anger
- Always on guard for an attacks from others

Non-Verbal Leak (NVL)

1. Eyes open
2. Eyes shiny and wide open
3. Difference between left/right side of mouth
4. Absence of concentration lines forehead (Botox?)
5. Pressure build up around the mouth
6. Tight top lip
7. Teeth showing
8. Disingenuous laugh
9. Mouth closed
10. Swallow down
11. Eyes open

Photo Courtesy of Gage Skidmore (Creative Commons)

Unconscious Meaning of the NVL

"I have pain it makes me angry, I can't show it, so I keep it inside, swallow it down and look for a hole in others logic that justifies me letting it out"

Symbolic Level of the NVL

SL-1 Shock, pain

SL-2 Anger in, sadness in

SL-3 Control by distancing and swallowing down

Five Reasons Why This Person Is a Type 2.1

- Eyes wide open
- Concentration lines
- Developed Masseter muscles
- Tension around mouth
- Jaw shifts

Personality Characteristics

- Capable of a Meta-level thinking
- Sends clear "two valued" messages
- Trustworthy and predictable regarding his views of reality
- Uninspired leader with power
- Analytical power that can "prove" his points well

Photo Courtesy of Gage Skidmore (Creative Commons)

- Can be prudent, and contemplative in the face of pressure
- Calculated risk-taker
- Can be stubborn and confrontational
- Thinker of feelings NOT a feeler of feelings
- Often misperceived as a powerful and very "feeling" person
- Mighty force to be reckoned with when logic is the issue
- Capacity to influence others with a blend of logic and feelings
- Natural negotiator who thinks he can win the negotiation
- Sought out for advice and judgment do to his skill and ability
- Doesn't trust ability to win with warmth so works harder to prove point with logic

Commentary Based on Public Presentations and Psychological Observation

Senator Rick Santorum is a very calculating person. What he lacks in humor he makes up for with his logic. He works hard at showing warmth. He is both affable and intelligent.

Photo Courtesy of Gage Skidmore (Creative Commons)

He is not afraid to take a moral stance on controversial issues. He is a quick study of others and is able to separate friend from foe easily. He is a quiet fighter using intellect logic and rhetoric to support and defend his viewpoints which are often seen as controversial.

Santorum revels in controversy and is often seen as an agent provocateur. This perception often held by others fits his self-concept well. He is a straight shooter whose gun shoots towards the left.

His somewhat rigid thinking and reluctance to acknowledge the possibility that others might be correct in their thinking, makes this former Senator vulnerable to people with strong logic and convincing information as well.

There is no doubt about his willingness to defend his arguments regardless of the consequences. Santorum is a man of character, honesty and integrity. His main problem is however his limited openness to difference.

This close mindedness has helped to hone him into a formidable opponent, with his right or wrong approach to difference, when his views and values are challenged. He is a polished package well-organized but maybe in need of a humor transplant.

Chapter 17

President Barack Obama

A CASE OF INSIGHT WITHOUT ACTION

Photo Courtesy of U.S. Government (Public Domain)

"There's not a liberal America and a conservative America. There's the United States of America."

Quote from keynote speech given at the 2000 Democratic National Convention

Background Information

Current Job	44th President of the United States of America
Previous Experience	• U.S. Senator from Illinois • He won the Nobel Peace Prize in 2009
Born	August 4, 1961
Birthplace	Honolulu, Hawaii (the first U.S. President not born in the continental United States)
Family	Wife: Michele Children: Malia and Sasha
Religion	Christian
Most Recent Book	*"Of Thee I Sing: A Letter to My Daughters"* (2010)
Cash on Hand (from Dec. report)	Hopes to raise at least the $750 million he did in 2008

Goodfield Personality Typing

Type 3.2 Inquisitor: "I am on my way, so get out of my way - please"

First impressions
- Presidential
- Great communicator
- Natural and comfortable with people
- Logical and convincing
- Self confident and self assured
- Clear power stated convincingly

- Likable, even when you disagree
- Gentleman

Statement of the NVL

1. Eyes open
2. Eyes shiny
3. Shifting of jaws
4. Eyebrow(s) up
5. Increasing pressure build up around mouth
6. Mouth open
7. Showing teeth
8. Mouth closed
9. Eyes closing, but not completely (distrust)
10. Swallow down
11. Eyes open

Photo Courtesy of U. S. Government (Public Domain)

Unconscious Meaning of the NVL

"I will look, reflect, hold in, position myself and then speak what I think I feel. I think my feelings that help me manage pain and anger. "

Non-Verbal Leak (NVL)

SL-1 Pain

SL-2 Anger in, sadness in

SL-3 Control by intellectualization and CER

Five Reasons Why This Person Is a Type 3

- One eyebrow up
- Shifting of jaws (smoking behavior)
- Eyes closing, but not completely (distrust)
- Difference between left and right side of mouth
- Blocked breathing

Personality Characteristics

- Intense
- Focused
- Distrusting
- Determined
- Persuasive
- Tough Strong
- Self-assured
- Often hostile
- Calm in crises
- Reveling controversy
- Arrogant
- Attracted to power
- Power to influence
- Self-concept "winner"
- History of risk taking
- Intelligent and educated

Photo Courtesy of Joe Crimmings Photography
(Creative Commons)

- Comfortable leadership skills
- Quintessential leader
- Relentless questioner

Barack Obama under Stress

Under stress Obama blocks his breathing and is in a mild trance. He has a flat affect which is seen in very shallow breathing.

He has a stance of head up and held on an upward left angle. It is an observer role. Always watching, waiting, assessing, and preparing with this thought, "Organize, fight, win!"

He can maintain calm which gives real insight into his basic strategy under stress. When the pressure around his mouth is increasing, it shows signs that his tongue is about to come out, indicating stress and blocked aggression.

Commentary Based on Public Presentations and Psychological Observation

As the President of the United States, who has served more than half of his term, Barack Obama warrants extended discussion.

Photo Courtesy of Utenriksdepartementet UD (Creative Commons)

Two wars, a troubled economy, devastating midterm elections which sent him a critical message and changed the power base in the Congress, it is fair to say, this President has been fully vetted.

The video showing President Obama watching the US Navy Seals assault the compound of Osama bin Laden provided the ultimate picture of the President's reaction to stress.

What we saw was a man pensive, withdrawn into his own thoughts, and acutely focused on the events of here and now.

Not a surprise, given the circumstances, but revealing just the same. Characteristic of his non-verbal response we saw a man blocking his breathing, controlling his movements and acutely aware of the circumstances going on around him. There was basically no discussion going on in the video clip provided by the White House. It is safe to say that the silence spoke volumes.

President Obama was in a cocoon of cautious consideration. What does it say about this man? There is a basic principle in psychology which says with stress goes regression. Under stress people tend to return to earlier learned patterns of behavior.

The increasingly cautious, graying fox in the White House showed this behavior in the debates on his road to the White House. He stands in a statuesque fashion with a somewhat rigid posture, looking, evaluating, planning, preparing and then responding when he is ready. His planned spontaneity provides insight into his decision making style.

President Obama is an active listener who may appear to not be listening. Few comments and reactions slip by him. Regardless of how one feels about his politics, it is correct to say, he may not like the stresses of the job but he has developed a successful means of dealing with the challenges he faces on a daily basis.

He is the President. He is doing what he believes to be in the best interest of the American people, regardless of the increasing public response, which seems to be telling him that he is on the wrong path.

As we saw him in the Situation Room of the White House, we see him behaving in his daily activity the same way. He will not be deterred; he will seek solutions in the same way as he has in the past. His self-concept is that of a person who is capable of negotiating the non-negotiable. His early history in Chicago and later in his early political career supports this psychological data base.

Whoever emerges, as the designated standard bearer for the Republican Party, Obama will be ready to meet that person with the same style that he used to defeat his biggest debating opponent Hillary Clinton. An internet review of that debate in Iowa would serve as useful homework to the next Republican Presidential candidate, who faces this seasoned opponent with a silver tongue.

Photo Courtesy of James O'Malley (Creative Commons)

Who will be our next President?

Chapter 18

Psychological Commentary and Closing Thoughts

A word to the wise –none would doubt that it is a daunting task to secure their party's nomination as the choice for the White House. After having successfully secured the right to take on the most powerful person, holding the most powerful job in the world, one would do well to accurately evaluate the tools they have in relationship to the job at hand.

President Obama is bright, informed, and possesses the most accurate and immediate data about the United States, and its relationship to the rest of the world. You may argue that Ronald Reagan, Bill Clinton, or any other former President was the most convincing speaker and debater. President Obama has clearly demonstrated outstanding skills in this area on personal, national and international levels.

The "contender" entering the Presidential ring must therefore, be informed, articulate and ready for the fight of their life.

It will take more than a pretty face and good intentions to win the White House. It will take more than saying change is necessary. It will take a believable plan stated in an understandable way to a doubting public.

The currency offered to any voter is and always has been two words, hope and change. These two words imply risk taking behavior and moreover, face the person who asks for their vote.

As much as there is chaos, confusion and carnage in our world today, in virtually all levels of human existence, people resist change. The American people will need more than a promise of "A chicken in every pot and a car in every garage". (Herbert Hoover 1928)

The politicians of today are dealing with a much more sophisticated constituency with social tools, such as the Internet, Facebook, Twitter, YouTube, LinkedIn etc. What has not changed is human behavior.

Regardless of the changes, we basically are the same people as our parents and grandparents and those before them. It seems to me that there are some striking parallels between what Tom Brokaw called, "The Greatest Generation" and our generation today.

Call it recession or depression, no one would argue, that times are tough. It is not just within our borders it is a worldwide problem.

There is a 24/7 news cycle that puts the plight of people right in our face before we go to bed and the moment we wake up. The message sent to us provides critical and important information about natural disaster, human conflict, and tragic human events. Our ancestors, at best, only read world events, if they ever heard about them at all.

We cannot escape the 24/7 news paradigm, in fact some of us have become addicted to our favorite network or "talking head" and doomsday predictors. This behavior is as addictive as cell phones and video games are to our teenagers. Regardless of their political bands for personal persuasion, their message remains the same, their analysis and interpretation varies significantly from left to right.

That message simply expresses the unfortunate and undeniable truth. We are powerless to affect the course of our own life and that of our family. One could argue that in the past ignorance was bliss. There is no such thing as blissful ignorance with a 24/7 news cycle.

The consequence of this is constant low-grade anxiety. It afflicts a population struggling with personal survival issues on a daily basis. The politician of today must try to make sense to an increasingly informed and skeptical population. This problem is addressed with three solutions: lies, damn lies, and statistics.

As cynical as this may sound, this remark acknowledges the good news and bad news of our time. We live in a sea of stimulus that floods our minds and affects our feelings.

There is good news however when considering the parallels we faced in the Depression and during World War II. Both periods reflected tough economic realities and families pulling together for their common good. There were people going off to war with the loss and tragedy that implied.

Patriotism has become a popular position held towards an all voluntary military service. The number of men and women regularly signing up for additional tours of duty reflects their belief, not necessarily in American foreign policy, but a belief in the plight of their comrades and the cause for which they fight and die. This is patriotism with wheels on. Involvement, genuine commitment is what America was about in the Depression and in World War II. It is also the America of 2011 and 12.

The views and values expressed by Roosevelt and Churchill reflect the contemporary concerns of our population today. We want jobs, opportunity, and a chance to restore our belief in ourselves and our country.

The Presidential candidate who is able to convincingly and honestly provide hope and change in equal measure will be the next President of the United States. The flickering faith, in who we are as a people, will not return to a full flame giving warmth and light until the basic belief in our systems and its institutions become practical plug-in-able plans and not political platitudes.

Chapter 19

The Non-Verbal Leak

What is so special about the Non-Verbal Leak (NVL)?

It is observable, comprehensible, and verifiable and reflects the other half of our message, a half that we may not even know about ourselves. If we can learn to read and understand these powerful communications from the unconscious recesses of the personality, then a new source of deeper data is revealed. That information can change the way we see ourselves and others. This has implications for the person on the next pillow or the dictator across the border.

It is simply a formal introduction to a different language that we have all used our entire lives with varying degrees of success and consequence. We can learn to understand it and use it to our advantage. The NVL is the silent language of the unconscious, silent yet powerful; visible yet often consciously unseen, influential yet often denied. It seduces, sabotages, and subjugates us in our daily interactions with others. This book is a look at how it works and how it impacts us on all levels of life.

The Non-Verbal Leak can be learned as well as any other language can be learned. It is the other half of our own language. The NVL is a new yet familiar step into the human communication process. With these new tools many mysteries unravel and are revealed. Why some relationships are doomed from the moment that they started. Why we are masters at snatching failure from the jaws of success. Why we make ourselves sick or insane. When we can see - literally see the messages from the unconscious, we can truly become the masters of our own destiny.

Being able to more accurately read the messages from the unconscious does not mean that you will magically find success or happiness. It simply means that you will have a deeper understanding of yourself and those around you. That awareness tends to change lifes.

The microscope and telescope did not create that which was not there. They simply provided a closer look and that consequently changed the way we saw and lived our lives. The Non-Verbal Leak is simply another life viewing tool.

Many people profess to possess this skill. Arms crossed means hiding something. A leg moving up and down indicates aggression.

Yes and no. Just as "hasta la vista", may have one meaning when friends wave goodbye at the airport or another when uttered by Arnold Schwarzenegger as he blows up the airport.

Context determines meaning and perception determines reality. The context in which an event takes place provides the framework that is helpful to define the meaning of the event. In a situation where a team is losing badly one might say, "They are being killed." Simply put, we are talking comparatively about what is in relationship versus what is expected. Hence context determines meaning and perception determines reality because it reflects the facts as we see them; this does not mean that they capture all of what there is to see.

When we think of non-verbal behavior it is possible to have a very quick reaction that others around may not record on a conscious level, but might record as a feeling "tone" that could affect their translation of the overall message. Just as your own language patterns are unique to you, so it is with regards to your non-verbal language.

What is a Non-Verbal Leak?

The NVL is a repetitive, patterned movement from the shoulders up, reflecting an unresolved perceived trauma and manifesting an old decision or strategy from the past. It is a way of looking at the strategies that the individual presents in his total non-verbal behavior.

Definition of the Non-Verbal Leak

The Non-Verbal Leak (NVL) is an often extraordinarily rapid, repetitive, patterned series of movements.

- It is from the shoulders up

- It reflects an unresolved Perceived Traumatic Event (PTE)

- It manifests a decision and a strategy from the past

- A decision and strategy believed to have been appropriate at the time, but maladaptive here and now

- When we look at an NVL, we are looking at the other half of the message of the body

- The NVL is, by definition, a double message

Symbolic Level (SL) of the Non-Verbal Leak

There are three ways in which the Symbolic Level of the NVL is thought about when evaluating it to a symbolic level. By Symbolic Level is meant the level in which a deeper meaning can be ascribed to the actions shown on the observable non-verbal level. It is decoding the behavior in a way that provides a next step to rendering the deeper unconscious meaning shown in the Non-Verbal Leak.

There are three ways in which the Symbolic Level (SL) may be defined:

- *Impact:* The impact is the person's first recording of a stimulus entering his system.
- *Primary Emotion:* The primary emotion is how the person initially would like to respond to a perceived stimulus.
- *Coping strategy:* The coping strategy is as it suggests, is the ultimate way in which a person decided to react to a perceived event.

These three distinct elements are simply a way of decoding non-verbal responses into their unconscious symbolic meaning.

The Impact or SL1

Any Perceived Traumatic Event (PTE) that is real in the eyes of the person who experienced it. This shock to the system can be recorded on both levels of consciousness.

Moreover, impact upon the person on an intra-psychic, psycho-physiological or interpersonal level.

- Impact is any Perceived Traumatic Event, it is the original trauma.
- It is real in the eye of the person that experiences it.
- A crisis happens and this shock to the system can record on a conscious or at an unconscious level.
- The impact upon a person is on intra-psychic, socio-physiological or on an interpersonal level.

In The Goodfield Method we talk about six possibilities that can be an Impact (SL-1):

- Shock (eyes large),
- Trance (eyes that are unfocused, white under eyes.)
- Fear (tearing)
- Denial (eyes closing and sometimes one eye looking away)

- Disbelief (eyes closing, eyebrows up)
- Pain (tearing, turn away from)

The Primary Emotion or SL2

This is the first impulse that the person has to the Perceived Traumatic Event (PTE). It is what he really wants to do.

Primary Emotion can be:

- Anger
- Sadness

The Primary Coping Strategy or SL3

This is what the person actually *does*, it is not what he wants to do. It's the realization for the person that when he gives in to the feelings of what he wants to do, he could make the situation even worse. It's the compromise that works for him at that moment.

With time and similar perceptions of what his world is like, he develops similar strategies for similar situations.

So something happens (SL1), it's traumatic, and the first reaction (SL-2) to it, is to strike it out. But when you start thinking about striking it out you say to yourself: "Hey, if I do this I'm going to end up in a world of trouble." The goal (SL-3) is to establish balance and to restore homeostasis to the system.

The SL-3 is the person's basic strategy in dealing with those feelings in his life. There are numerous coping strategies including:

- Denial
- Trance,
- Anger in/out,
- Sadness
- Calculated Emotional Response (CER), Seduction
- Control or distancing using variations of the other six SL3's

Structural Reading of the Non-Verbal Leak

Understanding the picture

Integrity: Reading the NVL of an individual requires the highest standards of ethical behavior and integrity of the reader. He or she should be aware that the reader is looking deeply into a person, which can have enormous consequences for the person when it is not properly handled or communicated. This is the cornerstone of the Goodfield Method.

Reading the NVL requires that we have a face in front of us. The Goodfield Method uses video equipment with which the person's face is being recorded. Some "simple" questions are being asked. Equally, we can read the NVL from a still-frame, a static recorded NVL, be it a still-frame from a video, a photo or any other kind of registration.

Reading the NVL is organizing information that is available on the screen. Dividing this screen into four quadrants makes it easier process all the information.

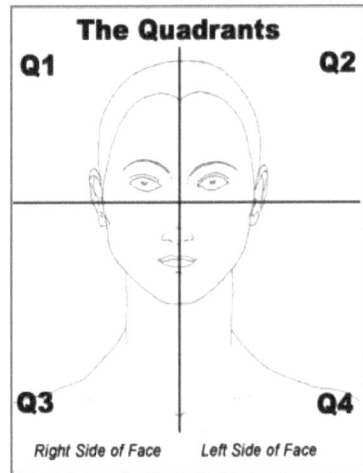

The Quadrants

Q1 Q2

Q3 Q4

Right Side of Face   Left Side of Face

Quadrants 1 and 3 are on the left side of the video and represent the right side of the individual. Q2 and Q4 are the right side of the video and represent the left side of the individual.

Most people in this world have an unfamiliar feeling when they see themselves on video or on photo. The reason is that individuals see themselves in the way other people are used to seeing them, but the image is just a turnaround from a mirrored image.

This unfamiliar image gives the individual an unnatural feeling that is nothing else than an encounter with himself. Here we meet the unconscious.

Want to learn the secret psychological underpinnings of candidates running for the U.S. Presidency? Learn their unique Non-Verbal Leak!

Chapter 20

Presidential Candidates by Goodfield Personality Type

The candidates are grouped by their personality type.

Name	Chapter	Personality	No.
Rick Perry	13	The Plotter	1.2
Michele Bachmann	2	The Thinker	2.1
Gary Johnson	9	The Thinker	2.1
Tim Pawlenty	12	The Thinker	2.1
Ron Paul	11	The Thinker	2.1
Rick Santorum	16	The Thinker	2.1
John Bolton	3	The Pouncer	2.3
Rudy Giuliani	7	The Pouncer	2.3
Sarah Palin	10	The Pouncer	2.3
Herman Cain	4	The Determinator	3.0
Newt Gingrich	6	The Determinator	3.0
Jon Huntsman	8	The Determinator	3.0
Charles E. Roemer III	14	The Determinator	3.0
Chris Christie	5	The Inquisitor	3.2
Mitt Romney	15	The Inquisitor	3.2
Barack Obama	17	The Inquisitor	3.2

Glossary

This glossary defines terms that are used in the Goodfield Method.

CER: Calculated Emotional Response

Definition of Report Level: Any behavior that is observable is testable. It is fact.

Impact: see SL1

Meta-level: being here and now. "No problem can be resolved on the level it began; you must see it from a 'helicopter view.'"

NVL Non-Verbal Leak: is an unconscious, repetitive, patterned movement from the shoulder up, and reflects an old decision or strategy from the past

Report Level: observations what literally can be seen (**first impression**)

Symbolic Level of Response: Observable behavior that is translated to a psychological level in terms of three factors:

⋏ **SL1: THE IMPACT:** How the person first perceives an event. It is real in the eyes of the person who experienced it. This shock to the system can be recorded on both levels of consciousness.

Moreover, it can impact upon the person on an intra-psychic, psychophysiological or interpersonal level as well.

⋏ **SL2: THE PRIMARY EMOTION:** The basic emotion wanted to be expressed. What the person intuitively wants to do.

⋏ **SL3: THE PRIMARY COPING STRATEGY:** What a person actually DOES, not necessarily the way s/he wants to express him/herself.

References

ABC Network and website

> Demographic details used to describe the candidate's background

Ames Straw Poll

> Far the most prominent of the several straw polls held in Iowa. Thus it is also commonly known as the *Iowa Straw Poll*. It was first held in 1979.

Associated Press website

> Demographic details used to describe the candidate's background

Brokaw, Tom

> *The Greatest Generation.* Random House Publishers, New York 1998

Chayefsky, Paddy

> *Network* 1976

Creative Commons
- http://creativecommons.org/
- Image courtesy of Gage Skidmore
- Image courtesy of Iowapolitics.com
- Image courtesy of Hoboken Condos
- Image courtesy of Mark Taylor
- Image courtesy of Jason Bedrick
- Image courtesy of Bill Fish - Victory NH
- Image courtesy of David Keller
- Image courtesy of World Economic Forum
- Image courtesy of Roger H. Goun
- Image courtesy of Marc Nozell
- Image courtesy of Bruce Tuten
- Image courtesy of Joe Crimmings Photography

- Image courtesy of James O'Malley

Fox News

Freud. Sigmund

Fragment of an Analysis of a Case of Hysteria, 1905

Gingrich. Newt

Announcement video May 11, 2011

GMA

May 13 & 23, June 6, 2011

Goodfield, Barry Austin

Insight & Action: The role of the unconscious in crisis from the personal to international levels. University of Westminster Press, London 1999

http://www.goodfieldinstitute.com/store.html

Goodfield, Barry Austin

"Process for Diagnosing and Treating a Psychological Condition or Assigning a Personality Classification to an Individual" Twelve Goodfield Personalities Types. United States Patent Application no. 12/124,938

Goodfield, Barry Austin

"Process for treating psychophysiological condition Inventor(s)" US3991744 Serial No. 570403, Filed 19750422, Issued 19761116

Goodfield, Barry Austin

"Minding Milosevic's Mind" Forensic Examiner Summer 2006

http://www.goodfieldinstitute.com/store.html

Goodfield, Barry Austin

"Saddam Hussein: The Unconscious Mind of the Butcher of Baghdad" Examiner Summer 2007

http://www.goodfieldinstitute.com/store.html

Hoover, Herbert

"A chicken in every pot and a car in every garage."

Presidential Campaign Slogan 1928

Huffington Post Website

Demographic details used to describe the candidate's background

Klein, Aron.

WABC radio talk show November 2010

New York Times Website

Demographic details used to describe the candidate's background

Obama. Barack

2000 Democratic National Convention: *"There's not a liberal America and a conservative America. There's the United States of America."*

Lenin, Vladmir

Doveryai no proveryai or "Trust but verify"

Progress Ohio (Public Domain)

Image courtesy

Schwarzenegger, Arnold

Terminator 2: Judgment Day 1991

Top Line

January & March 2011

US Government (Public Domain)

Image courtesy

130

USDA (Public Domain)

Image courtesy

Utenriksdepartementet UD (Public Domain)

Image courtesy

Wikipedia

Willie Nelson

Song "Mammas don't let your Babies grow up to be Cowboys"

"He ain't wrong he's just different.

About the Author

Prof. Barry Austin Goodfield, Ph.D., DABFM is Founding Director of The Goodfield Institute LLC in Glendale, Arizona, and the Netherlands. He holds a Ph.D. in Psychology and Human Behavior. In 1996 he became President & CEO of The Goodfield Foundation: for the Study of Conflict Communication and Peace Building. In 2010 he became President & CEO of The Goodfield Media Group International LLC.

Dr. Goodfield is also a Senior Professor at Henley-Putnam University instructing doctoral level students from the intelligence and counterterrorism community. He is a Family, Marriage and Child Therapist, international lecturer, author and noted radio and television personality. While a visiting Professor at the Diplomatic Academy of London he wrote the book *Insight and Action: The role of the Unconscious in crisis from the personal to international level*s University of Westminster Press, London 1999. *Relationships: A Survival Guide* (to be released Dec. 2011)

Prof. Goodfield holds two US patents on his psychotherapeutic process relating to analyzing the Non-Verbal Leak (NVL). He shared the Goodfield Method with psychiatrists, psychologists, social workers, senior corporate executives, attorneys, and cabinet level official around the globe.

Various international bodies such as the United Nations (ICTY) and NATO H.Q. Brussels, as well as governments such as the former Soviet Union, The Netherlands, Lithuania, Uzbekistan, Sri Lanka, Sultanate of Oman, Ukraine and Austrian Government have utilized the services and methodology of the Goodfield Institute and Goodfield Foundation.

Dr. Goodfield is a member of the following organizations:

- Diplomat, American Board of Forensic Examiners
- Diplomat, American Board of Forensic Medicine
- Diplomat, American Board of Psychology Specialists, Clinical Psychology
- Diplomat, American Academy of Experts in Traumatic Stress
- Diplomat, National Center for Crisis Management
- Member, American Psychological Association
- Member, American Federation of Television and Radio Artists
- Member, California Association of Marriage and Family Therapist
- Member, International Society of Police Surgeons, Inc.
- Member, Parliamentarians Network for Conflict Prevention
- Member, Phoenix Committee on Foreign Relations

Websites

www.goodfieldinstitute.com

www.goodfieldinstituut.nl

Find Dr. Goodfield on Facebook: on.fb.me/ub26Qa